Family Hikes in
Upstate South Carolina

Family Hikes in
Upstate South Carolina

Scott Lynch

milestone
press

almond, nc

Copyright © 2012 by Scott Lynch
All rights reserved
Second printing December 2013

Milestone Press, Inc., PO Box 158, Almond, NC 28702
www.milestonepress.com

Book design by Design Den www.designden.com & Jim Parham

Cover photos by Jim Parham and Mary Ellen Hammond
Interior photos by the author except as follows: Jim Parham pp. 41, 49, 53;
Mary Ellen Hammond pp. 37, 46

Cover photo: Twin Falls, Pickens County, South Carolina

Library of Congress Cataloging-In-Publication Data

Lynch, Scott, 1973-
    Family hikes in upstate South Carolina / Scott Lynch.
        p. cm.
    Includes index.
    ISBN 978-1-889596-25-9 (alk. paper)
    1. Hiking—South Carolina—Guidebooks. 2. Family recreation—South
Carolina—Guidebooks. 3. South Carolina—Guidebooks. I. Title.
    GV199.42.S58L96 2012
    796.5109757--dc23
                                2011052623

Printed and bound in the United States of America

*This book is sold with the understanding that the author and publisher assume
no legal responsibility for the completeness or accuracy of this book, nor for any
damages incurred while attempting any of the activities or visiting any of the
destinations described within it. The text is based on information available at the time
of publication.*

This book is dedicated to John Muir, who said,
"…the woods are calling, and I must go!"

Table of Contents

Introduction

Hiking is fun! It's simple, it's easy, and almost anyone can do it. Short, family-oriented hikes like the ones in this book don't require a lot of planning, packing, or preparation. Just about all it takes is a trail to blaze and some enthusiasm for the outdoors. What's more, hiking with your family is a special kind of outing. You'll be amazed at what fun your kids and, older family members, too, can have on a simple walk in the woods.

South Carolina is a small state with three general regions. The coastal area is called the "low country," the central piedmont is known as the "midlands," and the mountain section is referred to as the "upstate." For the purposes of this book, "Upstate South Carolina" includes the mountain and foothill counties of Oconee, Pickens, Greenville, Spartanburg, and Cherokee. Scattered across them is an assortment of state parks, natural areas, heritage trust preserves, national forests, and county parks. These tracts make up the bulk of the public land in the Upstate, and they are where you'll find the designated hiking trails—more than 140 of them. They vary in distance, terrain, elevation gain, and difficulty, and they offer plenty of opportunities for family hiking.

Due to the region's temperate climate, you can hike in the Upstate almost every day of the year. With an average winter daytime temperature in the 50s and summertime highs in the 90s, there's nearly always an opportunity for a family hike, whether it's a casual stroll or a multi-mile trek. However, always be sure to check the weather forecast before you head out—you're in the mountains, after all.

In the heat of summer, be sure to choose a hike near water. It's always cooler close to streams, and you might decide to take a dip. It's also a good idea to go early in the day—really early—before things heat up. On those rare icy days of winter, steer clear of waterfalls and other wet places where a slip could, at the very least, take all the fun out of a hike. Otherwise, winter is a great time to be in the woods. With no leaves on the trees and clearer air, the views are spectacular. Spring is the best time for seeing wildflowers, and at times an entire forest floor can appear to be in bloom. Plus, an early spring hike is a good cure for the winter doldrums. Fall brings its own spectacular color, with the tree leaves putting on their final show of the season. Entire mountainsides turn to a golden brown with spots of bright yellows and reds. No matter which hike you choose or what time of year, you're bound to have a good time.

This book is more than a list of available trails. Rather, it's a collection of complete hikes—the 20 best short hikes for families in the region. Each one starts and ends in the same place and may incorporate several trails. In addition, each one meets the following requirements:

- Location in one of the five Upstate South Carolina counties
- Round trip hiking distance of less than 4 miles
- Total time commitment of less than 2 hours
- Rated "Easy" or "Moderate" by the South Carolina State Trails Program (www.sctrails.net)
- Highlights like waterfalls, scenic views, historic buildings, interesting plant life, creeks, and pools for wading
- Minimum overall danger level, including exposure to fast moving water, uneven footing, steep inclines or declines, obstacles, etc.
- How the trail might change if sudden inclement weather arose (for example, how difficult it would be to return to your vehicle with children in a sudden downpour)

Timing is important when planning a hike, especially when the group includes younger children or older adults. The best hike plans go something like this: pack your gear the night before, eat a good breakfast, and pack a lunch at home before you depart. Arrive at the trailhead early in the day, allowing you to hike in the morning (which also happens to be the best time of day to take pictures). Eat lunch on the trail, and head back in the early afternoon. First thing in the morning everyone is fresh for hiking, and in the warmer months you'll avoid the hottest time of the day. A plan that has you finished hiking and back to your car shortly after lunch means you have many hours of daylight left should you run into any unexpected delays on the trail or driving home.

Physical fitness is another factor. Although almost all the routes listed here are rated easy or moderate in difficulty, always consider the fitness of everyone in your group when selecting a hike. Most can be enjoyed by just about anyone in reasonable physical condition, but a few will be challenging for older children and adults with average to above-average fitness. If you're not ready to hike one that's challenging, start with something easy and work up to it. Also, keep in mind that the number of stops and supervision required increase with a larger group. Know your family's limits and just go have fun!

So, what are you waiting for? Turn a few pages, find a hike or two that look good to you, dig through your closet for hiking shoes, load up the kids, and head out. In these days of "virtual" experiences, blazing the trails offers your family an interesting, healthful, low cost, and truly natural activity that's yours for the taking. Best of all, you'll be creating experiences and memories to last a lifetime. Happy hiking—see you on the trail!

How to Use This Guide

Hikes in this book are divided into sections based on the five counties of Upstate South Carolina: Oconee, Pickens, Greenville, Spartanburg and Cherokee. They are arranged from west to east across the state, starting with Oconee County and ending with Cherokee County. Within each county, hikes are grouped together based on proximity to one another.

Each hike entry has two photos to give you an idea of what to expect on the hike. Of course, once you're there you'll see much more. Taking photos of the scenery and of your family is one of the pleasures of hiking. When planning an outing, you might want to select a hike based on its geographical location, difficulty rating, or the hike summary. To make your selection easier, consult the *Hike Difficulty Index* and *More Trail Information* sections located in the back of the book.

Once you've chosen, read through the entire hike description, paying careful attention to the *Hiking Directions*. This will provide clues to the hike's character, unique features, and photo opportunities. Remember to carry this book with you for reference. Each hike entry includes the following information:

Summary	A general description of the hike, highlighting the most interesting features
General Location	Lists the approximate location in the county, and/or a reference to the nearest city
Hike Type	Trail configuration—Loop, Out & Back, etc.
Length	The distance hiked in miles, *always listed as round trip*. It is a good idea to preface any mention of trail distances with the term "approximately." When hiking with children, no one ever hikes the same distance. Going back and forth on the trail is the norm, and short side-trail excursions are not uncommon, either.
Time Commitment	The estimated hiking time for the trail described, when hiking the trail with a younger child. Add time for hiking with the smallest of children, and subtract time for older children. Does not include time for lunch or extended rest stops.
Difficulty	Each hike is classified as easy, moderate, strenuous, or some combination thereof (e.g. easy to moderate).

This rating is based on the effort required for a younger child, so what's moderate for a 6 year old is going to be easy for a pre-teenage child. For more information, consult the *Hike Difficulty Index* in the back of this book.

Trail Surface Describes the surface of the footpath you'll be hiking, including whether or not the trail is suitable for those with mobility impairments

Trail Traffic Provides information on trail traffic—for example, how likely you are to run into others on the trail

Best Hiking Season If there's a particular time of the year that's best to visit, it's listed here

Facilities Covers the availability of restrooms, drinking water, and picnic areas

Fee Most areas do not assess fees, but some do; South Carolina state parks have nominal fees (keep in mind fees are subject to frequent change)

Hours It is advisable to hike with children during daylight hours only. However, if a certain park, preserve, or trail has use restrictions, they are listed here.

Trail Markings Notes the color of blazes and/or markers, or whether there are no markings at all. If there are no markers, the ease of trail navigation is noted.

For More Info Lists the land management agency that can provide additional information about the trail(s)

Driving Directions How to get to the beginning of the trail by car from the nearest large city or community

GPS Coordinates Latitude and longitude for the trailhead parking area, given in decimal degrees for ease of entry for portable or car-based systems

Hiking Directions This is the "meat" of the trail information, including turns, ascents, descents, dangers, point-to-point hiking time estimates, and the best opportunities for family photos

Safety and Other Considerations

Regardless of the difficulty of a hike, always pack a hiking kit with the basics. Ensure that adults and older children know the contents and how to use them. These items will not take up much room in the family leader's backpack.

- First aid kit
- Matches; windproof and waterproof in a waterproof container. Also pack an inexpensive disposable lighter.
- Compass & map (if available); know how to use them
- Headlamp or flashlight
- Extra batteries
- Multi-tool or pocket knife
- Whistle
- Emergency blanket or bivy
- Toilet paper (place in a plastic baggie to avoid shredding)
- Trash bag
- Extra snacks and water

The Whistle

Each member in your hiking party should carry an emergency whistle. Just about any whistle will do, but there are excellent brightly colored "pealess" whistles, available at any sporting goods store, that generate about three times as much sound as the ordinary coach's whistle. They can be attached to a backpack or belt loops with small carabiners. The whistle can be useful if your family gets separated or if someone gets into trouble. The international distress call with a whistle is three loud, one-second blows. Practice this distress call with your family.

Common Sense for Avoiding Problems

- Avoid dehydration by drinking sufficient amounts of water and other fluids throughout the day. Bring a full day's worth of fluids for each member of your family. For younger children, plan on at least 24 ounces of water; for older children and adults, plan on at least 32 to 48 ounces. Drink more in warm weather, if you are sweating a lot, or if you are on an extended hike.
- It's a good idea to bring along snack food for each group member, in case you get caught out on the trail longer than you planned.
- Sunburn can occur in the winter as well as the summer. Apply a

sun block with a strong SPF rating and wear a wide-brimmed hat.
- In the warmer months, apply adequate insect repellent, preferably something without DEET. Also bring an ointment to treat bug bites.
- Sprained ankles can be avoided by wearing well-fitting shoes with good ankle support. Woolen socks or wool-synthetic blend are preferable to cotton even in summer, since cotton does not wick moisture from the skin.
- If serious injuries occur, send one person in your hiking group for help. Do not attempt to move a seriously injured person.
- Always dress sensibly and for any kind of weather. Unless it's the height of summer, remember to carry a light rain jacket or windbreaker, since weather is highly changeable in the mountains.
- Even the smallest children can carry a small backpack with their own windbreaker and snacks.
- Stay on marked trails. This will not only minimize hazards to you, but also prevent damage to the many delicate ecosystems in Upstate South Carolina.
- As the adult or leader of your family hiking group, behave in a mature and safe manner at all times. Be aware of your surroundings and look ahead for potential problems.

Hiking With Dogs

Many families like to bring their canine "best friend" along on a hike, but keep in mind that not everyone loves dogs. Hiking with a dog can be fun, but it does carry some risks. If you choose to bring your dog, be sure to:
- Call ahead to learn if dogs are allowed on the trail you plan to hike. If not, choose a different hike or leave Fido at home.
- *Always, always* keep your dog on a leash. An untethered dog can be very scary to many people—and, it's irresponsible.
- If possible, when meeting other hikers, stand off the trail with your dog and let them pass. Do not let your dog bark. People are on the trail to enjoy the sounds of nature.
- Scoop the poop and dispose of it properly.
- Make sure your dog's vaccinations are current and carry copies with you.
- Bring enough food and water for your dog, too.

Oconee County

South Carolina

1 Station Cove Falls

at Oconee Station State Historic Site

Enjoy a calm stroll through a hardwood forest and nearby wetlands, ending with a spectacular stepped, 60-foot waterfall. It's a great spot for a picnic.

Station Cove Falls is your destination on this hike.

General Location	7.5 miles northeast of Walhalla
Hike Type	Out & Back
Length	2 miles
Time Commitment	1.5 hours, minimum
Difficulty	Easy
Trail Surface	Natural surface, not suitable for those with mobility impairments
Trail Traffic	Light
Best Hiking Season	Year-round
Facilities	Restrooms and water are available at the Oconee Station State Historic Site during operating hours (Thursday through Sunday 9 am to 6 pm, closed January and February); there are several convenience stores and gas stations nearby on SC 11
Fees	None

Hours	No official restrictions, but hiking is advisable during daylight hours only
Trail Markings	Yellow blazes
For More Info	Sumter National Forest Andrew Pickens Ranger District 112 Andrew Pickens Circle Mountain Rest, SC 29664 864-638-9568

Directions to the Trailhead

★ =Start

1. From Walhalla, drive north 3.5 miles on SC 183 and turn left (north) on SC 11.

2. Continue on SC 11 for 1.5 miles and turn left on Oconee Station Road (S-95). You'll see a sign for Oconee Station State Historic Site.

3. Drive 2.4 miles (about a quarter-mile past the Oconee Station State Historic Site) to a trailhead on the left. Parking is limited; additional parking is available at the historic site picnic area.

Hiking Directions

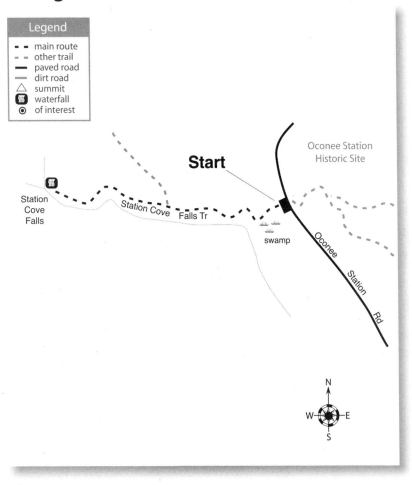

1. From the parking area, begin your hike to the left and behind the large trailhead information board.

2. Start a slow descent through a hardwood forest.

3. The trail will curve a couple of times before arriving at the foot of the hillside and following the edge of a marsh to your left.

4. Over the next 0.4 mile, you will cross three footbridges.

5. At 0.6 mile, you'll come upon a split in the trail with sign reading "Falls 300 Yards." Take the trail to the left, passing through a split-rail fence, to head towards the falls. Make sure children are not running ahead before this section.

It would be easy for youngsters to take the more well-worn right fork leading to Oconee State Park.

6. Hike another few hundred yards and navigate over rocks, crossing Station Creek.

7. Turn right after crossing Station Creek, walk another hundred yards, and you're at the beautiful 60-foot Station Cove Falls.

8. Return the same way you came.

Did You Know?

Oconee Station Historic Site is named for the stone blockhouse which stood at the edge of South Carolina's western frontier. It was used as a military outpost from about 1792 to 1799, then became part of a trading post compound established in 1805.

You'll cross Station Creek three times on footbridges.

with Licklog Falls plus the Chattooga River

This easy, 30-minute trek on the Foothills Trail to a divided waterfall, is just a hop and a skip from the Chattooga River. During the summer, children can splash and play in the pool below the falls.

Pigpen Falls is located on the Foothills Trail.

General Location	15 miles northwest of Walhalla
Hike Type	Out & Back
Length	2 miles; the hike can be slightly longer depending on how far you trek down to Chattooga River Trail
Time Commitment	2 hours, minimum
Difficulty	Moderate, due to the slight inclines on the way back to your car
Trail Surface	Natural surface, not suitable for those with mobility impairments
Trail Traffic	Can be crowded, especially in the summertime
Best Hiking Season	Year-round
Facilities	None; Oconee State Park is less than 4 miles away
Fees	None
Hours	No official restrictions, but hiking is advisable during daylight hours only

Trail Markings The first part of the hike is the white-blazed Foothills Trail; Chattooga River Trail is blazed black

For More Info Sumter National Forest
Andrew Pickens Ranger District
112 Andrew Pickens Circle
Mountain Rest, SC 29664
864-638-9568

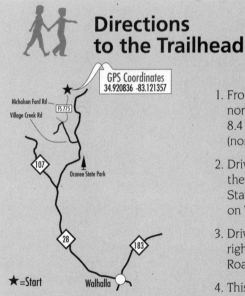

Directions to the Trailhead

GPS Coordinates 34.920836 -83.121357

1. From Walhalla, drive northwest on SC 28 for 8.4 miles and turn right (north) on SC 107.

2. Drive 3.1 miles, passing the entrance to Oconee State Park, and turn left on Village Creek Road.

3. Drive 1.7 miles and turn right on Nicholson Ford Road (FS 775).

4. This road is gravel and fords a couple of trickling brooks. Vehicles with low clearance could have difficulty crossing these after heavy rains.

5. Drive 2.2 miles on Nicholson Ford Road to a parking area.

Hiking Directions

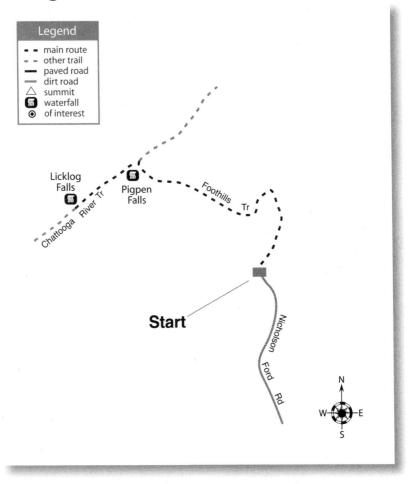

1. From the parking area, begin on the Foothills Trail to the left of the information board.

2. The trail starts a slow, winding descent into the Chattooga River corridor.

3. Walk 15 to 20 minutes (approximately 0.5 mile). Pass several open camping areas and cross two footbridges.

4. Soon you'll hear rushing water and see Pigpen Falls about 40 vertical feet down a trail to your left. You'll also see a longer footbridge just beyond and in front of the falls.

5. Ascend Chattooga River Trail. Enjoy Pigpen Falls and the pool where kids can splash and play.

6. Return the way you came.

Variation

7. From Pigpen Falls, cross the footbridge and hike another 5 to 10 minutes on Chattooga River Trail.

8. Arrive at Licklog Falls on your right. Use caution near the top and on the banks of the falls.

9. If you continue a little farther, you'll arrive at a spur trail leading down to the banks of the Chattooga. Following this trail to the river is well worth the little extra effort.

10. Retrace your steps to return to the trailhead.

Did You Know?

In 1974 the Chattooga River was designated a National Wild and Scenic River and its corridor protected from development in perpetuity. It was one of the first rivers to be so named.

Section I of the Chattooga River. This view looks south.

3 Bear Cove Trail
at Devils Fork State Park

Bear Cove Trail may be the toughest trail in this collection of hikes, but the mountain views from Lake Jocassee are worth the effort. It's a great hike for adventurous parents and healthy children over eight years old.

The view northwest across Lake Jocassee.

General Location	18 miles north of Walhalla
Hike Type	Loop
Length	2 miles
Time Commitment	1.5 hours
Difficulty	Strenuous, due to the many steep and rugged ascents
Trail Surface	Natural surface, not suitable for those with mobility impairments
Trail Traffic	Light to moderate
Best Hiking Season	Year-round
Facilities	Restrooms, water, and picnic shelters are available throughout the park
Fees	Park entry fee: $2 adults; free for children 15 and under; $1.25 SC seniors
Hours	8 am to 9 pm, however, hiking is advisable during daylight hours only

Trail Markings	White blazes. Pay close attention to them; there are many turns. The trail follows several old roadbeds and it would be easy to continue walking down a well-worn path and miss a turn.
For More Info	Devils Fork State Park 161 Holcombe Circle Salem, SC 29676 864-944-2639

Directions to the Trailhead

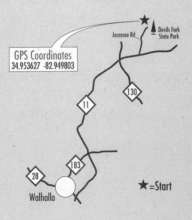

1. From Walhalla, drive north 13.5 miles on SC 11 and turn left on Jocassee Road (S37-25).

2. Drive approximately 4 miles on Jocassee Road. You'll begin to see signs for Devils Fork State Park.

3. Turn left at the first Devils Fork State Park entrance. This is the camping area entrance.

4. Turn right at the first drive and enter the parking area.

Hiking Directions

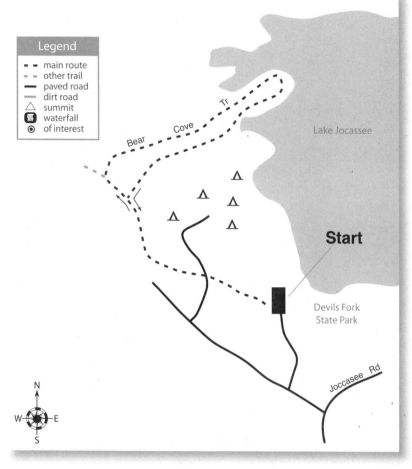

1. Bear Cove trailhead is located at the bottom end of the parking lot, directly below the restroom/picnic facility (Do not take the path that begins as an asphalt trail from the parking lot).

2. The trail descends slowly into a mixed hardwood and pine forest.

3. At 0.1 mile, cross a small footbridge over a trickling creek.

4. Beyond the footbridge 150 feet, the trail takes a sharp left turn away from creek and continues a short but steep climb to the road.

5. Cross the road and continue on the trail. Watch for white blazes

and directional arrow signs on the trees.

6. The trail winds again through forest for another 0.2 mile and turns left on an old roadbed.

7. After 0.1 mile, the trail turns right on another old roadbed.

8. For next 0.3 mile, the trail winds up and over several short but steep hills.

9. Cross a second small footbridge (with railing).

10. The trail begins to trace cliffs above Lake Jocassee. There are a couple of side paths that lead to the edge of the cliffs. These are not recommended; some of them are sheer 40-foot drops to the jagged rocks along the shores of Jocassee.

11. There is an obvious easy access point to the lake that is an excellent family photo opportunity. During the summer, with proper footwear, everyone can wade and play in the water.

12. After your photo and fun in the lake, return to the trail.

13. There is a bench near the lakeshore before the trail turns away from the lake and begins several more strenuous climbs.

14. At 1.7 miles, the route closes the loop at one of the old roadbeds you first traversed.

15. You have just 0.3 mile to go. Return to the parking area the way you came.

Jagged, weathered rocks line the shore of Lake Jocassee.

4 Oconee Bells
Nature Trail at Devils Fork State Park

An appealing stroll into a calm valley with many creek crossings and waterfalls, this hike showcases the vastness of Lake Jocassee and its surrounding mountains.

Start of Oconee Bells Nature Trail.

General Location	18 miles north of Walhalla
Hike Type	Loop
Length	1 mile
Time Commitment	1 hour
Difficulty	Moderate, due to a few hills
Trail Surface	Natural surface, not suitable for those with mobility impairments
Trail Traffic	Ranges from light in the winter to heavy in warmer weather
Best Hiking Season	Year-round
Facilities	Restrooms, water, and picnic shelters are available throughout the park
Fees	Park entry fee: $2 adults; free for children 15 and under; $1.25 SC seniors

Hours	8 am to 9 pm; however, hiking is advisable during daylight hours only
Trail Markings	White blazes; easy to follow
For More Info	Devils Fork State Park 161 Holcombe Circle Salem, SC 29676 864-944-2639

Directions to the Trailhead

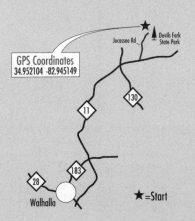

1. From Walhalla, drive north 13.5 miles on SC 11 and turn left on Jocassee Road (S37-25).

2. Drive approximately 4 miles on Jocassee Road. You'll begin to see signs for Devils Fork State Park.

3. Do not turn left at the camping entrance.

4. Bear right at the sign pointing to the park office and boat area.

5. Park in the area behind and below the park office.

Hiking Directions

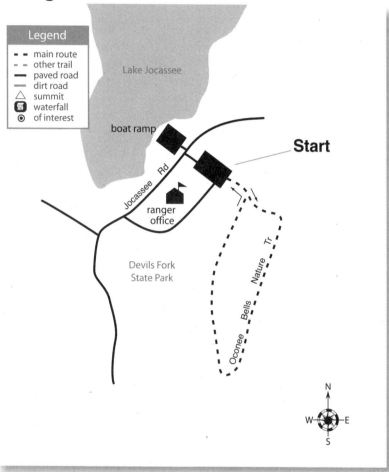

1. The trailhead is located at the large information board in the upper part of the parking lot.

2. Descend wide steps, then the trail turns left.

3. After 100 feet turn right, and the trail begins to wind back to the right.

4. At 0.1 mile, walk down three steps and the trail heads left, beginning a slow descent into the forest.

5. Walk down three more steps. From this point the trail parallels a beautiful, quiet creek for over half the length of the hike.

6. At 0.3 mile, cross a 15-foot bridge.

7. At 0.4 mile, cross a second bridge. There is a small, calm waterfall off to the right before the bridge.

8. At 0.5 mile, cross a third footbridge. Just beyond it, there is a small bench where you can rest and catch your breath.

9. Pass a single split-rail fence. The trail curves to the left. Off to the right you'll hear the sound of another small waterfall.

10. Enter a thicket of mountain laurel.

11. At 0.7 mile, you'll reach a longer boardwalk, with a mountain pond to your right and a small marsh.

12. The trail continues to wind and begins a moderately steep ascent from the creek valley to close the loop.

Did You Know?

Oconee Bells Trail is named for the rare wildflower found in only a few locations in the North Carolina, South Carolina, and Georgia mountains. It blooms along the trail from mid-March to early April.

Quiet mountain pond on Oconee Bells Nature Trail.

5 Buzzard Roost Heritage Preserve

This mile-long loop on Buzzard Roost Mountain includes striking scenery with views for miles. It also offers the most private and remote hiking experience you'll find in this book.

Winter vista from the top of Buzzard Roost Mountain.

General Location:	12 miles west of Walhalla
Hike Type:	Loop
Length:	1+ mile
Time Commitment:	1 hour
Difficulty:	Moderate, not recommended for children under age 10 due to the remote and rugged nature of the trail; this is true wilderness
Trail Surface:	Natural surface, not suitable for those with mobility impairments
Trail Traffic:	A private hiking experience is nearly guaranteed
Best Hiking Season:	Year-round
Facilities:	None
Fees:	None
Hours:	No restrictions, however, hiking is advisable during daylight hours only

Trail Markings: Round chrome hiker symbols, black arrows, and Heritage Preserve trail markers. The trail is not difficult to navigate, but could be covered in leaves in winter and tends to get overgrown in summer, so watch for these markers.

For More Info: DNR Heritage Trust Program
P.O. Box 167
Columbia, SC 29202
803-734-3893

Directions to the Trailhead

★ =Start

GPS Coordinates
34.761768 -83.186036

1. From Walhalla, drive north on SC 28 for approximately 6 miles.

2. Turn left on Whetstone Road and drive 0.75 mile.

3. Turn left on Cassidy Bridge Road and drive 1 mile.

4. Turn left on the winding dirt and gravel Rich Mountain Road and drive 3.0 miles.

5. Turn left on Forest Service Road F7441 (indicated by a small green vertical marker on the right side of the road).

6. Slow down. This road is winding, one-way, and in some parts, steep.

7. Drive approximately 1 mile on FS7441 and you'll see a one-car pulloff on the right with a trailhead post (the post is not marked, but you'll know the spot when you get to it).

8. Park your vehicle. In the unusual event that there's another car parked at the pulloff, you can drive 0.1 mile farther to a large turnaround/parking area at the end of the road.

Hiking Directions

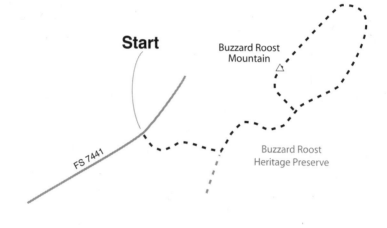

1. Begin your hike at the trailhead post.

2. The trail curves to the left and begins a short, steep descent. Wooden steps assist with your climb down. Beware of briar bushes in warmer months.

3. At the bottom of the hill is the official preserve signage with a topographical map of the area.

4. Turn left and begin hiking on the wide trail.

5. After about 100 yards, the trail turns left on an old roadbed.

6. At 0.15 mile, the trail turns right and begins a moderate ascent up and around the mountain.

7. At 0.3 mile, the trail begins to descend and bears left.

8. You'll come to a split in the trail where you can go straight, (fairly level), or take a sharp left (a steep climb up the side of the mountain). Go straight and continue winding around the mountain.

9. The trail curves to the left and begins a moderate ascent.

10. At just over a half-mile into your hike, you'll be at the top of Buzzard Roost Mountain. Stop and catch your breath, take in the views of the surrounding mountains and valleys, and snap a few family photos if you like.

11. Continue on the trail and begin the steepest descent of the hike. This is the climb you would have made if you'd gone left at step 8. It's also an option to turn around here and go back to the trailhead the way you came.

12. After your steep descent, turn right and return the same way you came.

Did You Know?

Buzzard Roost is home to other species of birds, too. Bring your binoculars to spy woodpeckers, warblers and rose-breasted grosbeaks. Black and turkey vultures also roost here occasionally.

Trail marker at Buzzard Roost Mountain. You'll also see round chrome hiker symbols and black arrows.

Pickens
County

South Carolina

6 Natural Bridge Trail
at Keowee-Toxaway State Natural Area

The landscape features of this challenging hike make it unique. Highlights include small waterfalls and pools, and a natural bridge over the creek—all in a hardwood forest studded with stands of lush mountain laurel.

Poe Creek cascades on Natural Bridge Trail.

General Location	20 miles north of Clemson, off SC 11
Hike Type	Loop
Length	1.5 miles
Time Commitment	1.5 hours to enjoy all this trek has to offer
Difficulty	Strenuous, but only because of a steep climb at the end; this trail is appropriate for all but the youngest children
Trail Surface	Natural surface, not suitable for those with mobility impairments
Trail Traffic	Light; this quiet trail is not well known
Best Hiking Season	Year-round
Facilities	Restrooms, water, and picnic shelters are available throughout the park
Fees	None
Hours	9 am to 6 pm Saturday through Thursday, 9 am to 8 pm on Friday; however, hiking is advisable during daylight hours only

Trail Markings	Small diamond-shaped signs on trees; the trail is easy to navigate
For More Info	Keowee-Toxaway State Natural Area 108 Residence Drive Sunset, SC 29685 864-868-2605

Directions to the Trailhead

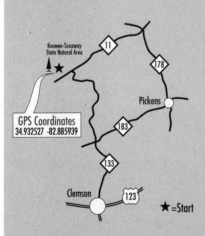

Keowee-Toxaway
State Natural Area

GPS Coordinates
34.932527 -82.885939

Pickens

Clemson

★ =Start

1. From Clemson, drive north on SC 133 for approximately 20 miles, where the road ends at SC 11.

2. Turn left on SC 11.

3. Immediately to your left, there will be a sign for Keowee-Toxaway State Natural Area. Do not turn here. This is the entrance for the interpretive center.

4. Continue past the Keowee-Toxaway sign and take the first right. This road is marked by a sign for camping, and is less than 0.1 mile from where SC 133 ended at SC 11.

5. Trailhead parking is at the Meeting House information center.

Hiking Directions

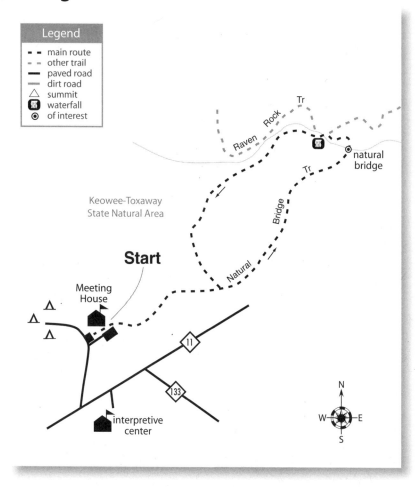

Legend
- **- -** main route
- **- -** other trail
- **—** paved road
- **—** dirt road
- △ summit
- 🌊 waterfall
- ⊙ of interest

Keowee-Toxaway
State Natural Area

Raven Rock Tr

natural
bridge

Tr

Natural Bridge

Start

Meeting
House

11

133

interpretive
center

N
W—⊕—E
S

1. From the parking area, begin the paved ascent past the Meeting House on your left.

2. Just past the Meeting House, you'll come to the official trailhead for both Natural Bridge and Raven Rock trails.

3. Sign in at the trail registry kiosk. This is required for hikers in the Keowee-Toxaway Natural Area.

4. The trail begins by winding through a hardwood forest over gently rolling hills.

5. Ten minutes into the hike, you'll hear the rushing waters of Poe Creek to your left.

6. The trail descends to the natural bridge after which it is named—a huge slab of rock across the creek.

7. The Poe Creek natural bridge is great place to stop for play. During the summer months, children can scramble under and around the bridge with caution, and splash in the water of the surrounding pools. Upstream a few yards to the right of the bridge are a couple of cavern/cave-type rock configurations. Explore this area; you're guaranteed to have fun. Photo opportunities here are excellent and unlike any other place featured in this book.

8. After enjoying the Poe Creek natural bridge, continue down the trail.

9. The trail curves around to the left, then comes to a split marking the way to Raven Rock. Continue straight on.

10. To your left, you'll hear more rushing water, and there's another opportunity for wading and water fun just a few feet away.

11. Continuing, you'll descend stairs to a creek crossing over large boulders.

12. From here you'll hike a couple of steep ascents and descents, finally moving away from Poe Creek and its tributaries.

13. Your final ascent is a real challenge, but it doesn't last more than 3 or 4 minutes.

14. Close the loop to meet the original path on which you began, and return to the trailhead the way you came.

The natural rock slab bridge that gives the trail its name.

Twin falls is the most photogenic destination in this book, with two segmented waterfalls cascading more than 75 feet. There are several places for kids to splash and play in Reedy Cove Creek and excellent opportunities for family photos.

Twin Falls is located just a quarter-mile from the trailhead.

General Location	15 miles north of Pickens, off US 178
Hike Type	Out & Back
Length	0.5 mile
Time Commitment	1 hour—the distance is short, but you'll want to enjoy it at a leisurely pace
Difficulty	Easy (the easiest hike in the book)
Trail Surface	Natural surface, suitable for those with mobility impairments and families with strollers
Trail Traffic	Heavy nearly year-round because of the waterfall attraction and easy access; for lighter traffic go Monday through Thursday
Best Hiking Season	Year-round, but be cautious about ice after a night of below-freezing temperatures
Facilities	None
Fees	None
Hours	Dawn to dusk

Trail Markings:	None—the trail is 10 to 15 feet wide for most of the hike and is easy to navigate
For More Info:	Felbern Foundation 1429 Highway 176 West Tryon, NC 28782 828-859-6745

Directions to the Trailhead

GPS Coordinates
35.008426 -82.823288

Waterfall Rd

Table Rock State Park

Cleo Chapman Rd

11

Eastotoe Community Rd

178

★=Start

Pickens

1. From Pickens, drive north on US 178 for approximately 9 miles until you reach SC 11 at the 4-way stop.

2. Continue driving north on US 178 for 3 more miles.

3. Turn left on Cleo Chapman Road. The famous Bob's Place Tavern is on the left.

4. Drive exactly 2 miles on Cleo Chapman Road. Be careful; this road is winding, steep, and damp most times of the year.

5. Turn right at a T-intersection on Eastotoe Community Road and drive 0.8 mile.

6. Turn right on Waterfall Road. This winding dirt and gravel road is mostly one lane, so stay alert and be careful.

7. Drive 0.3 mile to the end of the road and parking area.

Hiking Directions

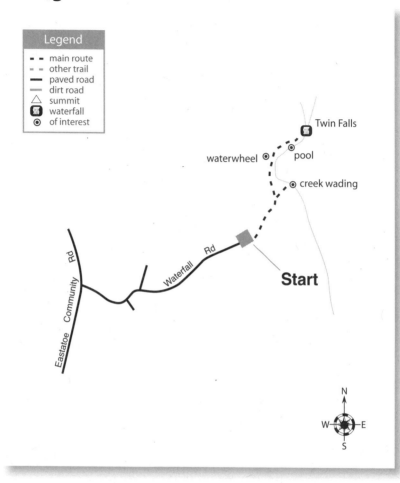

1. Begin your hike immediately beyond the parking area past the split-rail fence.

2. Walk on the flat, wide trail for approximately an eighth of a mile to a side trail heading down to Reedy Cove Creek.

3. Turn right on the side trail for summertime wading. This is a safe place for children (under adult supervision) to play in the water.

4. Continuing on the main route, there's a split-rail fence and waterwheel. This is a great spot for a family photo.

5. The trail begins a slight incline to the wooden steps and covered platform facing the impressive Twin Falls.

6. If you're adventurous, you can climb down to the massive rocks and navigate close to the falls. Use extreme caution; this is recommended for older children only. Here you can snap some of the best photos and get within a few feet of these colossal falls. It's also a great place for a family picnic.

7. After your waterfall adventure, retrace your steps to the trailhead.

Optional

8. On your return, just past the falls viewing area and beyond where the water rushes down a long slick stretch of rock, there's a large, calm, 3- to 5-foot swimming and wading pool off to the left of the trail. You probably saw it to your right on the way in. This is a great place for the entire family to take a dip on a hot summer day.

Did You Know?

Twin Falls, located at the head of the Eastatoee Creek Gorge, is also known locally as Reedy Cove Falls, Rock Falls, and Eastatoee Falls.

Reedy Cove Creek runs along Twin Falls Trail.

8 Glassy Mountain Heritage Preserve

An easy hike on the flanks of a solitary mountain, offering extraordinary views over miles of the surrounding Piedmont landscape. Large expanses of exposed granite along the way make great picnic spots.

View from the overlook on Glassy Mountain.

General Location	2 miles outside Pickens, off SC 183
Hike Type	Out & Back
Length	1 mile
Time Commitment	45 minutes
Difficulty	Easy to moderate
Trail Surface	Natural surface, not suitable for those with mobility impairments
Trail Traffic	Light to heavy, depending on the day of the week; go Monday through Thursday for the lightest traffic
Best Hiking Season	Year-round—however, because of roots over most of the trail, this hike is not recommended after rain
Facilities	None, but downtown Pickens is only 2 miles away
Fees	None
Hours	Dawn to dusk

Trail Markings	No official blazes, but the trail is obvious and has a few chrome hiker markers nailed to trees along the way
For More Info	Department of Natural Resources Heritage Trust Program P.O. Box 167 Columbia, SC 29202 803-734-3886

Directions to the Trailhead

★=Start

1. From downtown Pickens at the intersection of SC 8 and SC 183, drive east on SC 183 (Farrs Bridge Road) for 1.5 miles.

2. Turn left on South Glassy Mountain Road and drive 1 mile. Slow down; this road becomes very steep and has several sharp turns.

3. At the 1-mile point on South Glassy Mountain Road, you'll come to Glassy Mountain Church Road on your right. Just past this road approximately 150 feet, there's a small pulloff to the right with a trailhead indicator.

4. The pulloff has space for only a couple of vehicles, so if this spot is taken, park just across the road in another tiny pulloff or continue driving on South Glassy Mountain Road for another 0.2 mile to the top. Park here and walk back down to the trailhead.

Hiking Directions

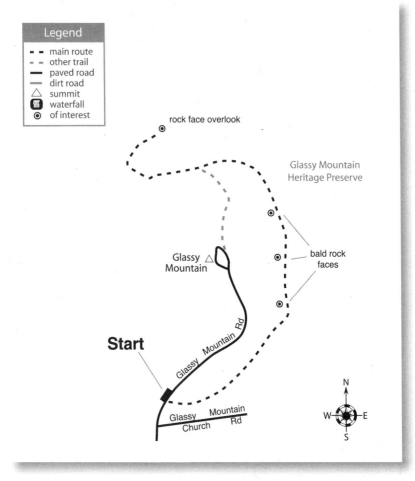

1. Begin your hike just beyond the parking area to the right of the trailhead information.

2. The trail starts out relatively flat and zigzags along the side of the mountain. Caution: the trail has many roots and rocks. Keep a close eye on young children.

3. Between 0.1 and 0.3 mile, there are three large exposed flat rock faces that are great places for family photos. They can be slippery when wet, however.

4. The trail continues to wind— although it never becomes strenuous—around the mountain.

5. At 0.4 mile, you'll come upon a split in the trail. Continue straight (the route goes slightly

right) and the trail will begin to descend.

6. Approximately 200 feet beyond the split, the trail switchbacks and descends to the right.

7. Walk another 150 feet to the final exposed rock face, which offers some of the best Piedmont views in the Upstate. This is a great place for photos, a good rest, and a picnic lunch.

8. Return to the trailhead the way you came.

Did You Know?

Glassy Mountain is a manadnock, an isolated knob or small mountain that rises from a relatively flat plain. It gets its name from small springs near the summit which trickle across expanses of exposed granite, making it appear shiny, or "glassy," from a distance.

Granite rock face on Glassy Mountain. The best overlook is at the turnaround point.

9 Hagood Mill Nature Trail

This charming walk for all ages includes a step back in time and a quiet mountain stream in a beautiful surrounding forest. Consider making the hike part of a larger tour of this restored historic site managed by Pickens County Museum.

Waterwheel at Hagood Mill. You'll see the mill as you start your hike.

General Location	3 miles north of Pickens, off US 178
Hike Type	Loop
Length	0.75 mile
Time Commitment	1 hour, minimum
Difficulty	Easy
Trail Surface	Natural surface, suitable for those with mobility impairments
Trail Traffic	Never crowded, but because of the popularity of the old Hagood Mill, you're almost guaranteed to see others
Best Hiking Season	Year-round
Facilities	Restrooms and water are available at the visitor center when it is open
Fees	None

Hours	Dusk to dawn; visitor center hours are Wednesday through Saturday, 10 am to 4 pm
Trail Markings	None—the trail is easy to follow
For More Info	Pickens County Museum 307 Johnston Street Pickens, SC 29671 864-898-5963

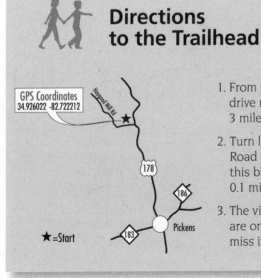

Directions to the Trailhead

GPS Coordinates
34.926022 -82.722212

★ =Start

1. From the city of Pickens, drive north on US 178 for 3 miles.

2. Turn left on Hagood Mill Road (take care making this blind turn) and drive 0.1 mile.

3. The visitor center and mill are on the right; you can't miss it.

Hiking Directions

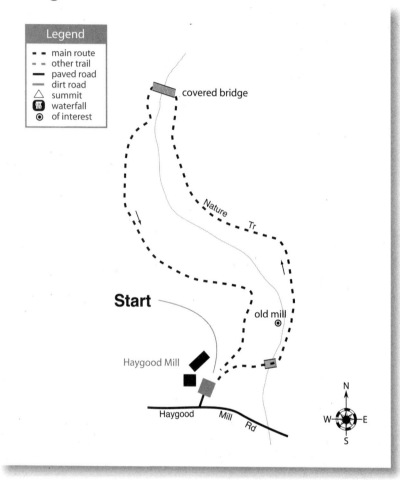

1. Begin your hike by walking toward the mill. This is the largest of three restored buildings and is on the right, next to the stream.

2. Just before the mill, cross the footbridge over the stream.

3. Turn left past the footbridge to officially begin the nature trail.

4. The trail ascends and wanders beyond the old mill, a great place for photographs.

5. For the next 0.1 mile, the trail follows the ridge above the stream.

6. At 0.3 mile, there's a bench where you can rest and enjoy the peaceful forest.

7. Just beyond the bench, you'll begin on an old roadbed.

8. At approximately 0.5 mile, you'll see a covered footbridge below and to your left. Make a hard left and descend to cross the footbridge. This is the only covered bridge in this book and another great location for pictures.

9. After the bridge, turn left and continue down the easy trail.

10. The remaining 0.2 mile takes you through the woods above the stream and returns you just beyond the three historical buildings where you began the hike.

Did You Know?

Hagood Mill, established circa 1845, is one of the oldest known surviving gristmills still producing grain products in South Carolina. On the third Saturday of each month it holds a free mini-festival, with events ranging from fiddling competitions and living history performances to arts workshops for kids.

Covered bridge along Hagood Mill Nature Trail. The bridge is located half-way around the loop.

Greenville County

South Carolina

Trail at Chandler Heritage Preserve

A *quiet walk in the forest with impressive views of the surrounding mountains, few crowds, and a pristine winding creek. This hike takes little time or effort in a quaint setting that's perfect for a picnic lunch.*

Eva Russell Chandler Trail follows Slickum Creek.

General Location	Just off US 276, 4 miles south of Caesars Head State Park
Hike Type	Loop
Length	0.5 mile
Time Commitment	30 minutes
Difficulty	Easy
Trail Surface	Natural surface, suitable for those with mobility impairments
Trail Traffic	Light; this trail is not well known
Best Hiking Season	Year-round, though the trail can be slippery after heavy rain or in winter after leaves have fallen
Facilities	None; water, restrooms, drink machines, snacks, and phones are available 4 miles farther on US 276 at Caesars Head State Park
Fees	None
Hours	Dawn to dusk

Trail Markings	No official marks or blazes; the trail is easily navigated
For More Info	Department of Natural Resources Heritage Trust Program P.O. Box 167 Columbia, SC 29202 803-734-3886 www.dnr.state.sc.us

Directions to the Trailhead

GPS Coordinates
35.084197 -82.607542

★=Start

1. From Greenville, drive north on US 276, passing through the towns of Travelers Rest, Marietta, and Cleveland.

2. Follow US 276 towards Caesars Head.

3. Once past intersection of US 276 and SC 8, continue on US 276 approximately 2.5 miles (you'll pass the popular Bald Rock lookout spot).

4. Slow down after passing Bald Rock lookout. Turn right onto a gravel road in a bend (Persimmon Ridge Road). Keep your eyes peeled; this road is easily missed.

5. Drive 0.7 mile, winding down the gravel road, and park at the pulloff on the right. Do not block the gate.

6. Note: Persimmon Ridge Road is a steep, gravel, one-lane road that may be difficult to navigate. However, it is passable by all vehicles; four-wheel drive is not required.

Hiking Directions

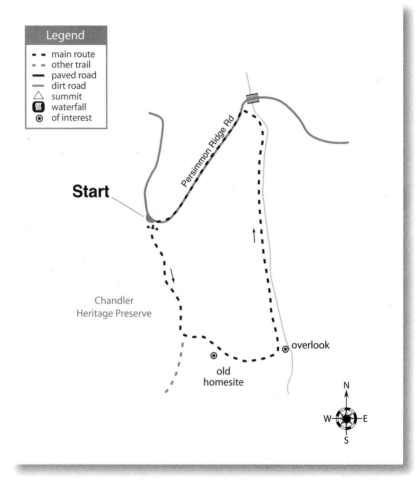

1. Pass through the gate and follow the old roadbed for approximately 200 feet.

2. Turn left and follow wooden steps onto the rail.

3. The trail curves to the left, passing old chimney remains, and then continues down, winding through mixed hardwood and pine.

4. In a few minutes, reach a bald rock overlook of a scenic mountain range. Be cautious when allowing children on the rock overlook; Slickum Creek spills down over the rock face and it can be very slippery.

5. After enjoying the view, continue on the trail past the top of the bald rock.

6. The trail turns left and continues through the quiet forest along winding Slickum Creek to meet Persimmon Ridge Road.

7. After you reach the road, look to your left; your parked vehicle is only a 3- to 4-minute walk away. Or, to extend your hike, you may return to the trailhead the way you came through the forest (recommended).

Did You Know?

Eva Russell Chandler Trail is a good place to spot wildflowers, from long-spurred violets in spring to grass-of-Parnassus in late fall. The 253-acre preserve protects several other rare plant species, including Indian paintbrush and thousand-leaf groundsel.

A sign marks the trailhead at Eva Russell Chandler Trail.

11 Blue Trail

at Asbury Hills United Methodist Youth Camp

This pleasing stroll around a mountain lake features a boardwalk, a marsh, and a camp amphitheater.

Asbury Hills Lake on Blue Trail.

General Location	Just off SC 276, south of Caesars Head State Park
Hike Type	Loop
Length	1 mile
Time Commitment	1 hour
Difficulty	Moderate, due to a couple of short but steep climbs
Trail Surface	Natural surface, not suitable for those with mobility impairments
Trail Traffic	Light in winter, very crowded in summer or at other times when camp is in session
Best Hiking Season	Year-round—however, the trail could be slippery after heavy rain, or after leaves have fallen in winter
Facilities	Restrooms and water spigots available at the camp
Fees	None, but call ahead to get permission to enter and use the trails; during the summer and other times when the camp is full you may not be allowed to hike there
Hours	Generally from dawn to dusk; ask about the camp schedule when you call

Trail Markings	None—the trail is 10 to 15 feet wide for most of the hike and easy to navigate
IMPORTANT	This trail is open to the public, but you must call ahead (864-836-3711) to get permission and the code to the entrance gate
For More Info	Asbury Hills United Methodist Youth Camp South Carolina United Methodist Conference 150 Asbury Drive Cleveland, SC 29635 864-836-3711 AsburyHills@umcsc.org

Directions to the Trailhead

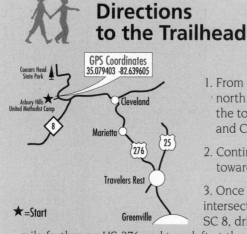

GPS Coordinates
35.079403 -82.639605

Caesars Head State Park

Asbury Hills United Methodist Camp

8

Cleveland

Marietta

276   25

Travelers Rest

★ =Start

Greenville

1. From Greenville, drive north on US 276, passing the towns of Marietta, and Cleveland.

2. Continue on US 276 toward Caesars Head.

3. Once past the intersection of US 276 and SC 8, drive approximately 1 mile farther on US 276 and turn left at the sign for Asbury Hills United Methodist Camp.

4. Continue down the road for 0.25 mile and keep right on Asbury Drive. Drive to the entry gate and enter your code.

5. Drive carefully into the camp, obeying the low speed limit. Remember, children could be anywhere! Drive all the way to the back of the camp.

6. A hundred yards past the archery range on the left, you'll see a well house with a sign reading, "Trail Head and Daily Use Information." Turn left past the well house and park.

Hiking Directions

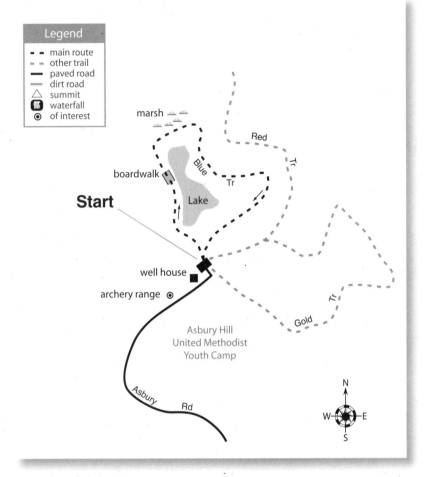

1. From the parking area, take the blue-blazed trail that branches to the left and ascends a hill.

2. The trail follows the shoreline and winds through a tunnel of thick rhododendron.

3. After 10 minutes of hiking along the lake, you'll arrive at a long boardwalk crossing a wetland area. If you look upstream from the wetland, you will see the towering Raven Cliffs. Exercise caution when crossing the boardwalk.

4. Ascend a good-sized hill and take the trail to the right, returning on the east side of the lake.

5. You'll pass an outdoor amphitheater and cross over a ridge into a densely wooded cove where a small creek winds through the forest.

6. To end your hike, either cross over the sandy dam of the lake, or follow Asbury Trail back to the parking area.

Did You Know?

Asbury Hills Camp & Retreat Center encompasses 2,000 acres and offers a wide variety of summer camp experiences for kids in elementary, junior high, and senior high school. The Center also offers retreat events and a place for custom retreats, serving churches, non-profit organizations, and the local community.

You'll cross the wetland section of Blue Trail on a boardwalk.

12 Lake Placid
at Paris Mountain State Park

A *quiet hike circling a charming lake in one of the Upstate's most popular and accessible state parks.*

Lake Placid at Paris Mountain State Park.

General Location	Just north of Greenville
Hike Type	Loop
Length	1.2 miles
Time Commitment	30 minutes
Difficulty	Easy
Trail Surface	Natural surface, suitable for those with mobility impairments
Trail Traffic	Can be crowded; for the lightest traffic, go Monday through Thursday
Best Hiking Season	Year-round
Facilities	Restrooms, water, and picnic shelters are available throughout the park
Fees	Park entry fee: adults $2, children 15 and under free, SC seniors $1.25
Hours	8 am to 9 pm; hiking is advisable during daylight hours only

Trail Markings	No official marks or blazes, but the trail is easily navigated
For More Info	Paris Mountain State Park 2401 State Park Road Greenville, SC 29609 864-244-5565 pmountainsp@scprt.com

Directions to the Trailhead

GPS Coordinates
34.926708 -82.369845

★ =Start

1. From I-385 in Greenville, take Exit 40.

2. Go north on SC 291 (Pleasantburg Drive) for 1.6 miles.

3. At US 29, take a hard left (west) to continue on SC 291.

4. After another 2.5 miles, turn right on SC 253 (State Park Road).

5. Continue 2.7 miles, turning left on SSR 344; you'll see signs for Paris Mountain State Park.

6. Drive approximately 1 mile on SSR 244 and the entrance to Paris Mountain State Park is on the left.

7. Once in the park, drive 0.2 mile until you see the park office down on your left. Park either adjacent to the office or across the street.

Hiking Directions

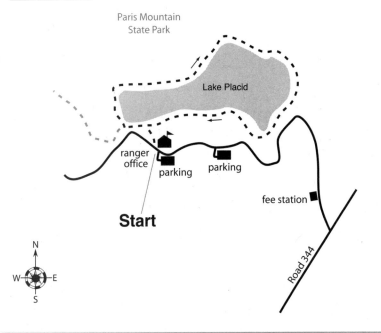

1. From the parking area, walk down to the stone park office.

2. Descend the stone steps on the porch side of the office.

3. Turn left at the fence and follow the signs for the nature trail.

4. Cross a footbridge.

5. Turn right at the nature trail sign, continuing on the trail.

6. The trail now follows the lake shore.

7. Cross a unique S-curve boardwalk—a great place to stop and skip rocks on the lake. You're now a third of the way through the hike.

8. At the lake's northern end (approximately the half-way point), descend stone steps

in front of the dam cascade. Watch your footing here. This is always a favorite family photo spot; you can even assist your children out into the water on the rocks and take some impressive photos of them in front of the dam.

9. Continue around the lake, passing the restroom and covered picnic area on a hill to your left.

10. Cross a long elevated bridge and turn right immediately after crossing (do not ascend steps to the left after the bridge).

11. Walk through a large picnic area; another restroom is to your left here.

12. At the far end of the picnic area, the trail splits. The right trail leads down to the lake recreation area.

13. Take the left trail to return to the park office and finish your hike.

Did You Know?

Lake Placid is a 15-acre body of water stocked with bream, bass and crappie. Canoes, kayaks and pedal boats are available for rent at the lake recreation area from Memorial Day through August.

Lake Placid dam, located half-way around the loop at the far end of the lake.

13 Mountain Creek Trail
at Paris Mountain State Park

A calm, easy trek that ambles past a marsh, along a quiet mountain stream, and through stands of mountain laurel.

Mountain Creek.

General Location	Just north of Greenville
Hike Type	Out & Back
Length	2.4 miles
Time Commitment	1.5 hours
Difficulty	Easy
Trail Surface	Natural surface, suitable for those with mobility impairments
Trail Traffic	Can be crowded; for the lightest traffic go Monday through Thursday
Best Hiking Season	Year-round
Facilities	Restrooms, water, and picnic shelters are available throughout the park
Fees	Park entry fee: adults $2; children 15 and under free; SC seniors $1.25
Hours	8 am to 9 pm; hiking is advisable during daylight hours only

Trail Markings	Orange blazes; the trail is not well blazed, but is easy to follow
For More Info	Paris Mountain State Park 2401 State Park Road Greenville, SC 29609 864-244-5565 pmountainsp@scprt.com

Directions to the Trailhead

GPS Coordinates
34.926708 -82.369845

★ =Start

1. From I-385 in Greenville, take Exit 40.

2. Go north on SC 291 (Pleasantburg Drive) for 1.6 miles.

3. At US 29, take a hard left (west) to continue on SC 291.

4. After another 2.5 miles, turn right on SC 253 (State Park Road).

5. Continue 2.7 miles, turning left on SSR 344; you'll see signs for Paris Mountain State Park.

6. Drive approximately 1 mile on SSR 244 and the entrance to Paris Mountain State Park is on the left.

7. Once in the park, drive 0.3 mile until you see the park office on your left. Park either at the park office or across the street.

Hiking Directions

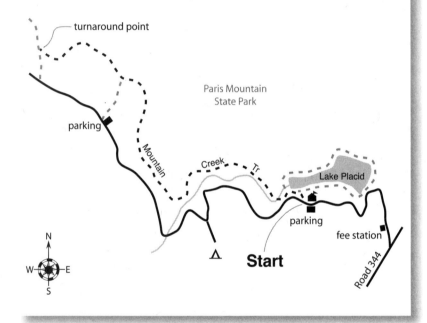

Legend
- - main route
- - other trail
— paved road
— dirt road
△ summit
▨ waterfall
◉ of interest

turnaround point

Paris Mountain
State Park

parking

Mountain

Creek

Tr

Lake Placid

parking

fee station

Road 344

N
W · E
S

△ **Start**

1. From the parking area, walk down to the stone park office.

2. Descend the stone steps on the porch side of the office.

3. Turn left at the fence and follow signs for the nature trail.

4. Cross the footbridge.

5. Turn left at the sign to begin Mountain Creek Trail.

6. Walk 100 yards and turn right onto the trail. From this point, the trail is considered multi-use and, except on Saturdays, is frequented by mountain bikers. Keep small children close by.

7. The trail wanders past a marsh to the left.

8. At 0.2 mile, the trail crosses an amphitheater area.

9. Beyond the amphitheater, the trail enters a hardwood forest, never straying too far from the creek for the first quarter-mile. There are numerous photo spots and even a picnic area along the creek.

10. The trail continues through the woods, winding gently up and down a few hills (it's never strenuous) until reaching the junction with Sulphur Springs Trail (this connecting trail is not recommended; it is strenuous by adult standards).

11. Turn around here and retrace your steps to the trailhead.

Did You Know?

Paris Mountain State Park was built during the Great Depression by the Civilian Conservation Corps. Today, a renovated bathhouse, now called the Park Center, is a hub for Park activities. It houses a 3-D map of the park, historical exhibits, and a nature classroom. In addition to activities at the Park Center, the Park is busy year-round with picnickers, hikers, and cyclists.

Mountain Creek. The trail stays close to the creek in the hardwoods.

14 Pleasant Ridge Nature
Trail at Pleasant Ridge County Park

This moderately challenging hike is well worth the drive to the trailhead. It begins with a short, strenuous climb through thick hardwoods dotted with interpretative signs, and ends at a simple playground and a few small waterfalls.

A rustic sign and footbridge mark the trailhead at Pleasant Ridge Nature Trail.

General Location	15 minutes north of Traveler's Rest on SC 11
Hike Type	Loop
Length	0.7 mile
Time Commitment	1 hour, minimum
Difficulty	Moderate to strenuous due to a couple of long, steep ascents, but suitable for all ages because of the short distance
Trail Surface	Natural surface, not suitable for those with mobility impairments
Trail Traffic	Light to moderate; this quiet trail is not well known
Best Hiking Season	Year-round, but steep ascents and descents could be slick when the ground is wet
Facilities	Restrooms, water, and picnic shelters are available throughout the park

Fees	None
Hours	Dawn to dusk
Trail Markings	Blue blazes; the blazes are few but the trail is easy to follow
For More Info	Pleasant Ridge County Park P.O. Box 2 Cleveland, SC 29635 864-836-6589

Directions to the Trailhead

GPS Coordinates
35.086818 -82.479419

Pleasant Ridge County Park

Cleveland

Marietta

Travelers Rest

Greenville

★=Start

1. From Greenville, drive north on US 25, passing through Travelers Rest.

2. About 10 minutes outside of Travelers Rest, turn left onto SC 11.

3. Drive approximately 2 miles on SC 11 until you see the signs for Pleasant Ridge County Park.

4. Turn right into the park.

5. Turn right at the first parking area.

Hiking Directions

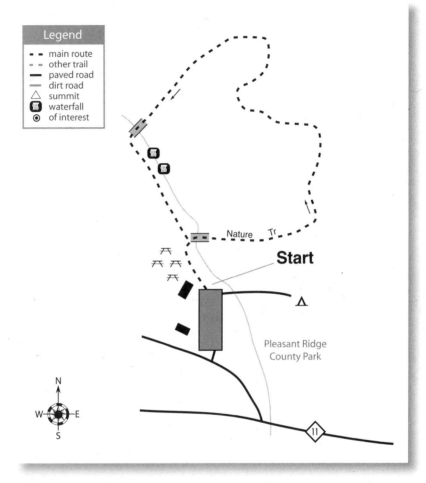

1. From the parking area, look toward the picnic area and you'll see a wooden sign indicating the direction of the nature trail.

2. Walk past the sign and through the grassy picnic area, cross the creek on a footbridge, and begin your hike at the trailhead marker.

3. Start a rutted, steep ascent that continues for over a quarter-mile.

4. Along the way you'll pass several informational signs where you can stop to catch your breath.

5. After your tough climb, you'll begin a descent into a thick wooded area near a stream.

6. After a sign marking an old moonshine still site, the trail splits. Turn right and go up a steep hill to enjoy a simple playground and views of the recreational pond. Continue straight along the creek to complete the trail.

7. Back on the trail (at creekside), cross a second footbridge.

8. After this footbridge, you'll be treated to a couple of small waterfalls that are great for wading and picture taking. There are several unofficial trails that scramble down to the falls.

9. After your waterfall fun, return to the trail. It's only a couple of minutes' walk to the end of the hike.

Did You Know?

Pleasant Ridge County Park was developed as a state park in the 1940s to promote tourism in the Upstate. It was originally established for the Black community, and Paris Mountain State Park was built for Whites. Both parks were integrated in the 1960s. Pleasant Ridge was turned over to the Greenville County Recreation District in 1985.

One of the small waterfalls near the end of the hike.

15 Bunched Arrowhead Heritage Preserve

If *you're looking to get away from crowds, this is the trail to blaze. It offers a quiet stroll through open fields, a hardwood forest where the path parallels a stream, and a marsh with several boardwalks.*

The trail at Bunched Arrowhead Heritage Preserve begins in a field.

General Location	2 miles east of Travelers Rest
Hike Type	Loop
Length	1.5 miles, approximately
Time Commitment	1 hour, minimum
Difficulty	Easy
Trail Surface	Natural surface, could be suitable for those with mobility impairments
Trail Traffic	Very light; you are almost guaranteed a solitary walk
Best Hiking Season	Year-round, but the ground can get quite soggy after many days of heavy rains
Facilities	None
Fees	None
Hours	Preserve gates are open from 7:30 am to 7:30 pm, April 1 through August 31; 8 am to 6 pm September through March

Trail Markings	No official blazes, but directional arrows on the trail make it easy to follow
For More Info	Department of Natural Resources Heritage Trust Program P.O. Box 167 Columbia, SC 29202 803-734-3886 www.dnr.state.sc.us

Directions to the Trailhead

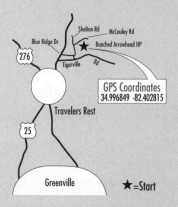

GPS Coordinates
34.996849 -82.402815

★ =Start

1. From Greenville, drive north on US 25 to Travelers Rest.

2. Pass through Travelers Rest, slowing down past the stop light at Tigerville Road.

3. Turn right onto Blue Ridge Drive.

4. Drive 0.7 mile and turn left onto Shelton Road.

5. Drive 0.8 mile and turn right on McCauley Road.

6. Drive 0.4 mile and the large parking lot for the Heritage Preserve is behind a long fence on your right.

Hiking Directions

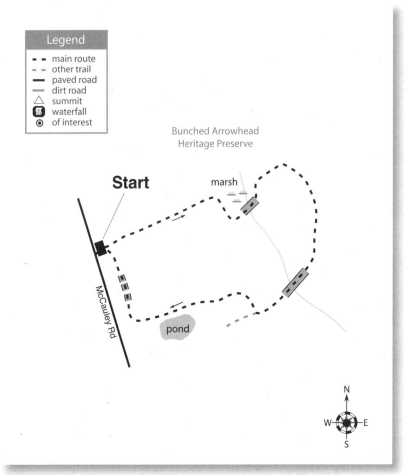

Bunched Arrowhead
Heritage Preserve

Start

marsh

McCauley Rd

pond

Legend

- – main route
- – other trail
- — paved road
- — dirt road
- △ summit
- ▨ waterfall
- ⊙ of interest

N
W—E
S

1. From the parking area, walk past the heritage preserve sign and begin a gradual descent in a field towards the woods.

2. Enter the woods and the trail turns right.

3. The trail emerges into a field and parallels woods on your left.

4. Descend into the forest with the creek to the left.

5. Pass marshland on your left in the forest.

6. Cross a 30-foot boardwalk—a great family photo opportunity.

7. The trail continues to wind through hardwood and pine forest for another 0.4 mile.

8. Cross a second boardwalk.

9. In less than 0.1 mile from the boardwalk, turn a hard right. Note: the trail appears to continue straight on; turn right. There is a small sign on a wooden post indicating the correct direction.

10. Walk straight down the wide path with a pond to your left. This is an excellent spot for skipping rocks.

11. The trail makes another hard right turn.

12. Cross a field.

13. Cross three more small boardwalks, all within 100 feet of each other.

14. A slow and easy 0.3-mile ascent skirting a field takes you back to the parking lot and ends the hike.

Did You Know?

The 179-acre Bunched Arrowhead Heritage Preserve was named after a plant it protects: the federally-endangered bunched arrowhead plant, *Sagittaria fasciculata*, which occurs in wetland seeps within rare Piedmont seepage forest. Other rare plants found here include climbing fern, *Lygodium palmatum*, and dwarf-flowered heartleaf, *Hexastylis naniflora*.

One of several boardwalks at Bunched Arrowhead Heritage Preserve.

Spartanburg County

South Carolina

16 Peters Creek Nature Preserve

The network of trails on this 142-acre preserve offers access to several creeks with water crossings and opportunities to wade.

A trailhead sign points the way at Peters Creek Nature Preserve.

General Location	Just west of Spartanburg, off I-85
Hike Type	Out & Back or Loop
Length	3.5+ miles of trails, with various options
Time Commitment	2 hours
Difficulty	Moderate, due to distance and a few hills
Trail Surface	Natural surface, not suitable for those with mobility impairments
Trail Traffic	Light; this quiet trail is not well known
Best Hiking Season	Year-round, but avoid this area after heavy rains; Peters Creek and Mineral Springs Creek will flood after heavy downpours, making water crossings treacherous
Facilities	None—there are several convenience stores/gas stations nearby on Cannons Campground Road and Gossett Road

Fees	None
Hours	Dawn to dusk
Trail Markings	The main trail is blazed red, but there's a blue-blazed trail as well
For More Info	Department of Natural Resources Heritage Trust Program 4037 India Hook Road Rock Hill, SC 29732 803-366-7024

Directions to the Trailhead

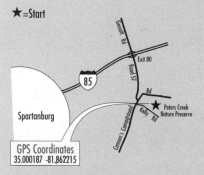

★ =Start

GPS Coordinates
35.000187 -81.862215

1. From I-85 in the Spartanburg area, take Exit 80 (Road 57).

2. Go south towards Converse to the first stop sign at Cannons Campground Road.

3. Turn right on Cannons Campground Road.

4. Drive less than .10 mile and turn left on Kelly Road.

5. Follow signs for Peters Creek Nature Preserve, driving 0.6 mile to a dirt/gravel road on the right. Turn right on this unnamed road.

6. The parking lot for the preserve is in the powerline right of way.

Hiking Directions

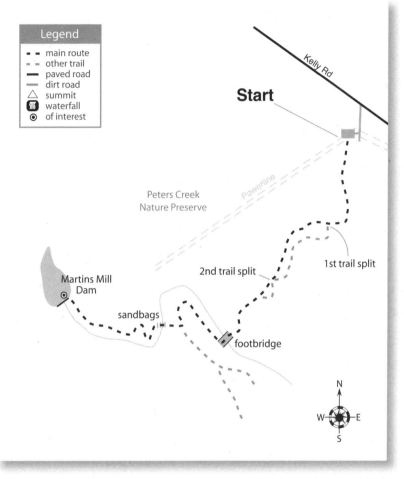

1. From the parking area, begin your hike to the left, behind the large trailhead information board.

2. At the trailhead there's a mailbox with trail maps. Take a map with you.

3. Start a slow descent through hardwoods.

4. After a few hundred yards, the trail will split. You can go either way, but to descend and head towards Peters Creek, turn right.

5. The trail follows a tributary of the creek only a few feet away on the right.

6. After a couple of hundred yards, the trail splits again. Go right again to head directly to Peters Creek.

7. Cross a footbridge.

8. Arrive at Peters Creek.

9. From here, you can cross the creek on sandbags, continue on the trail, and explore this nature preserve. There are several more easily navigated side trails, most of which intersect with the creeks.

10. To end the hike, return the same way you came.

Did You Know?

Peters Creek Nature Preserve is home to one of the largest communities on earth of the endangered dwarf-flowered heartleaf plant.

Peters Creek. Side trails intersect with this stream and its tributaries.

17 Pacolet River Heritage Preserve

Situated on the banks of the river from which it takes its name, the trail at this primitive, 270-acre nature preserve winds through mixed hardwoods and pines.

Pacolet River.

General Location	10 miles east of Spartanburg, off US 176
Hike Type	Out & Back
Length	1.5 miles
Time Commitment	1 hour, minimum
Difficulty	Moderate due to the steep climb away from the Pacolet River valley on the return
Trail Surface	Natural surface, not suitable for those with mobility impairments
Trail Traffic	Light; there are never more than 2 or 3 vehicles parked at the trailhead
Best Hiking Season	Year-round, but the steep descent to the river could be slippery after heavy rain
Facilities	None
Fees	None

Hours	Dawn to dusk
Trail Markings	No blazes, but the trail is marked with chrome arrow markers and easy to follow
For More Info	Department of Natural Resources Heritage Trust Program P.O. Box 167 Columbia, SC 29202 803-734-3886.

Directions to the Trailhead

★ =Start

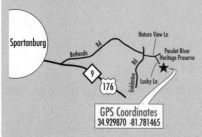

GPS Coordinates
34.929870 -81.781465

1. From Spartanburg, drive east on US 176/SC 9 approximately 6 miles.

2. Turn left on Bethesda Road and drive 3.6 miles.

3. Turn right on Goldmine Road and drive 0.3 mile.

4. Turn left on Nature View Lane and drive 0.1 mile.

5. Bear right on Lucky Lane. This is a dirt road.

6. Arrive at the trailhead parking lot 0.4 miles farther on Lucky Lane.

Hiking Directions

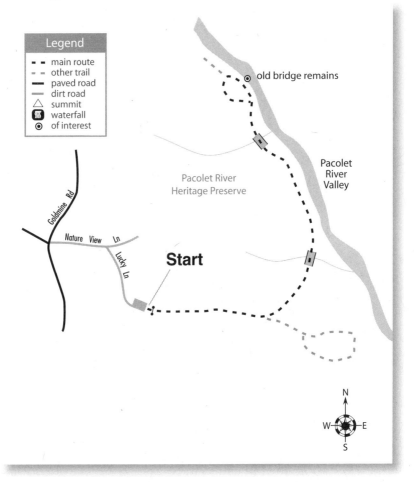

Legend
- – – main route
- – – other trail
- — paved road
- — dirt road
- △ summit
- 🌊 waterfall
- ◎ of interest

old bridge remains

Pacolet River
Heritage Preserve

Pacolet
River
Valley

Goldmine Rd

Nature View Ln

Lucky Ln

Start

N
W—✦—E
S

1. Pass through the gate and follow the old roadbed for 0.2 mile.

2. The trail curves to the left and descends slowly for 0.1 mile.

3. The descent continues steeply for several hundred feet. This could be slippery after rainfall.

4. Cross a footbridge and enter the Pacolet River corridor.

5. Within about 200 yards, reach the beautiful Pacolet River.

6. The trail follows the riverbanks for another 0.4 mile, crossing another footbridge.

7. Along the riverbank you'll pass interesting trees, vines, and canopy vegetation.

8. The main trail ends at the remains of the old bridge. This is the best turnaround point.

9. An extension trail begins immediately past the old bridge, but this is not recommended due to difficulty and the lack of trail markings.

10. Return to the trailhead the way you came.

Did You Know?

Pacolet River Heritage Trust Preserve protects two prehistoric soapstone quarries that date back 3,000 to 5,000 years.

You'll cross a footbridge as you enter the Pacolet River corridor.

18 Edwin M. Griffin Nature Preserve

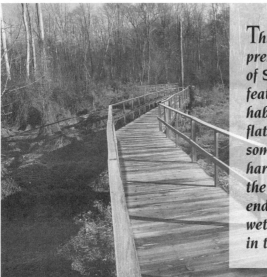

This easy-access preserve in the heart of Spartanburg features varying habitats. Its wide, flat trails traverse some of the largest hardwood forest in the Upstate and end at the longest wetland boardwalk in the county.

This boardwalk crosses the largest wetlands in Upstate South Carolina.

General Location	Just north of Greenville City of Spartanburg, eastside
Hike Type	Out & Back or Loop
Length	3+ miles of trails with various options; recommended route is approximately 2 miles
Time Commitment	1.5 hours, minimum
Difficulty	Easy
Trail Surface	Natural surface, suitable for those with mobility impairments
Trail Traffic	Can be quite crowded with locals walking or trail running; go Monday through Thursday for the lightest traffic
Best Hiking Season	Year-round
Facilities	None
Fees	None
Hours	Dawn to dusk

Trail Markings	No blazes; there are a few trail signs throughout the preserve and trails are easy to navigate
For More Info	S.P.A.C.E. P.O. Box 18168 Spartanburg, SC 29304 864-948-0000 www.spartanburgconservation.org.

Directions to the Trailhead

★ =Start

1. From I-26 in Spartanburg, drive east on US 29 approximately 6 miles. You will pass through the west side of Spartanburg, the downtown area, and well beyond Converse College.

2. Turn right on Fernwood Drive and continue 0.5 mile **past** the first Beechwood Drive.

3. Turn left on the second Beechwood Drive. Park in the lot immediately to your right.

Hiking Directions

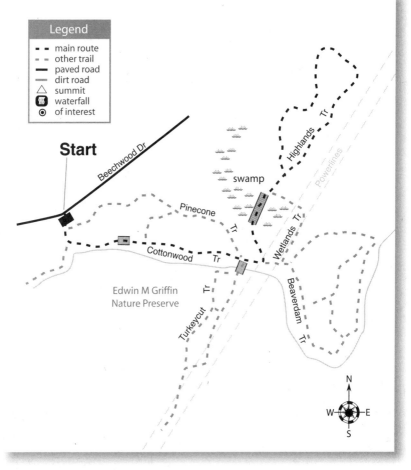

1. Begin beyond the trailhead sign, following Cottonwood Trail. This trail circles the preserve.

2. The wide trail curves to the left and crosses a footbridge.

3. Turn left after the footbridge (turning right takes you to another parking area on Syndor Road).

4. The trail follows the elevated banks of Lawsons Fork Creek for 0.3 mile. There is a bench here overlooking the creek.

5. Immediately after a long footbridge crossing Lawsons Fork Creek, you'll see signs for "Wetlands."

6. Turn left and enter the wetlands.

7. The trail continues over a swamp on the longest boardwalk in Spartanburg County. This is a real treat for the kids and a great picture opportunity; they will be standing over a real wetland habitat. Benches are situated at intervals along the boardwalk.

8. Leaving the boardwalk, continue straight as you enter a hardwood forest.

9. Turn around at any point in the forest and retrace your steps to the trailhead, or continue on this more than 3-mile loop that takes you back to the parking area.

Did You Know?

Edwin M. Griffin Nature Preserve is an important water quality buffer in a fast-growing region and provides habitat for myriad plants and animals. On its more than five miles of signed trails you may see deer, wild turkey, fox, beaver, and raccoon, along with many birds, reptiles, and wildflowers. Preserve signs identify more than 50 species of trees.

Beyond the wetlands, the trail enters a hardwood forest.

19 Croft Nature Trail
at Croft State Natural Area

A *hilly wilderness loop hike featuring hardwoods and the beautiful rocky banks of Fairforest Creek. The remains of a half-century-old bridge add interest near the end of the walk.*

Fairforest Creek along Croft Nature Trail.

General Location	10 miles southeast of Spartenburg, off SC 56
Hike Type	Loop
Length	1.5 miles
Time Commitment	1 hour, minimum
Difficulty	Moderate
Trail Surface	Natural surface, not suitable for those with mobility impairments
Trail Traffic	Light to moderate; bicycles and horses are not permitted, so this trail does not see as much traffic as the many others
Best Hiking Season	Year-round
Facilities	Restrooms, water, and picnic shelters available throughout park
Fees	Park entry fee: adults $2; children 15 and under free; SC seniors $1.25
Hours	Dawn to dusk

Trail Markings	Blue blazes
For More Info	Croft State Park 40 Croft State Park Road Spartanburg, SC, 29302 864-585-2913 (summer) 864-585-1283 (winter)

Directions to the Trailhead

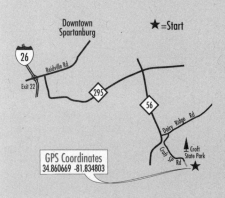

1. From exit 22 on I-26 in Spartanburg, drive east on Reidville Road and turn right (south) on SC 295 for 7 miles.

2. Turn right (south) on SC 56 and drive 3 miles.

3. Turn left on Dairy Ridge Road and drive 0.3 mile.

4. Turn right on Croft State Park Road and drive 3.3 miles until you reach the park office, which will be on the left.

5. Drive past the park office; the road turns to dirt here. Park immediately on the left at the equestrian arena area parking.

Hiking Directions

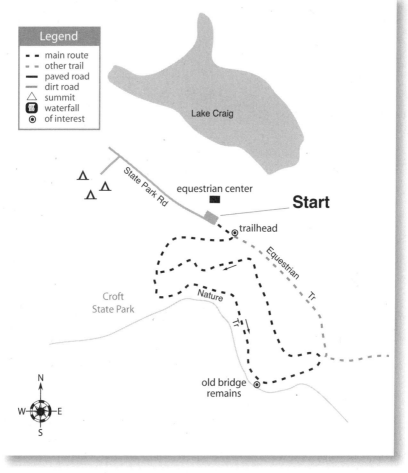

1. From the parking lot, turn left onto the dirt road and walk 0.2 mile until you reach the nature trail sign on a split-rail fence.

2. Begin an easy stroll through a pine forest, winding to the left and right a couple of times.

3. At 0.2 mile, the trail splits. Go right to descend to the Fairforest Creek bottomland.

4. At 0.4 mile, the trail joins the banks of Fairforest Creek. This beautiful rock-strewn stream, so large it could be called a river, has some nice photo opportunities. You'll encounter many side trails leading to the water.

5. Continue along the banks for 50 yards, descend three steps,

and follow the trail as it takes a hard left (it will seem you should go straight forward, but turn left!).

6. The trail ascends slightly away from the creek and crosses several small boardwalk bridges.

7. Soon you'll see a double blue blaze, cautioning you to pay attention to the trail as it makes a hard left. Looking to your right, you'll see the remains of an old vehicle bridge over Fairforest Creek. This is a good photo opportunity but take care if you venture near the bridge ruins.

8. Begin a sometimes steep ascent out and away from Fairforest Creek, winding back up to the split you encountered at the beginning of the hike.

9. Bear right to return to the trailhead.

10. At the trailhead, turn left and walk 0.2 mile on the dirt road to reach your car and end the hike.

Did You Know?

Once an Army training base, Croft State Natural Area comprises nearly 12 miles of rolling, wooded terrain that also provides habitat for a wide variety of flora and fauna—just five miles from downtown Spartanburg.

A split-rail fence marks the nature trail at Croft State Natural Area.

Cherokee County

South Carolina

20 Cowpens Nature Trail
at Cowpens National Battlefield

A *dense bamboo thicket caps off this easy loop hike that winds through hardwoods and features a stream with several bridge crossings.*

The "enchanted" bamboo forest on Cowpens Nature Trail.

General Location	15 miles northeast of Spartanburg, off SC 11
Hike Type	Loop
Length	2 miles
Time Commitment	1 hour
Difficulty	Easy
Trail Surface	Natural surface, suitable for those with mobility impairments
Trail Traffic	Can be quite crowded; for the lightest traffic, go Monday through Thursday
Best Hiking Season	Year-round
Facilities	Restrooms, water and picnic shelters are available throughout the park
Fees	None
Hours	9 am to 5 pm daily, except holidays

Trail Markings	No blazes, but the trail is well marked with a directional sign at every quarter-mile
For More Info	Cowpens National Battlefield National Park Service P.O. Box 308 Chesnee, SC 29322 864-461-2828

Directions
to the Trailhead

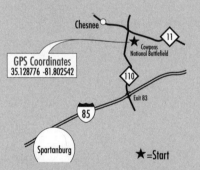

GPS Coordinates
35.128776 -81.802542

★ =Start

1. From I-85 east of the Spartanburg area, take Exit 83 and turn left (north) on SC 110.

2. Drive 6 miles and turn right on SC 11.

3. Drive 0.5 mile and turn right into entrance to Cowpens National Battlefield. (Ignore the sign instructing you to drive another mile on SC 11 to reach the "Trailhead Parking.")

4. Drive 0.4 mile to the visitor center on your left.

5. Stop at the visitor center and pick up a map.

6. Turn left out of visitor center parking lot and drive 1.3 miles to the picnic area.

7. Turn right into the picnic area and park.

Hiking Directions

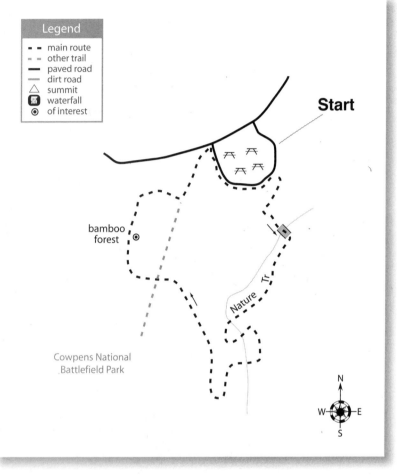

Legend

- - main route
- - other trail
— paved road
— dirt road
△ summit
▨ waterfall
◉ of interest

Start

bamboo forest ◉

Cowpens National Battlefield Park

Nature Tr.

N
W — E
S

1. From the parking area, walk past the large group picnic shelter. The trail begins off to your left in the curve of the road.

2. The trail immediately turns right and begins a gradual winding descent into a hardwood forest.

3. At 0.15 mile, cross a footbridge.

4. The trail winds through hardwoods. There are mileage/directional signs every quarter-mile on the trail.

5. At approximately 0.5 mile, cross the creek.

6. Continue through the forest, crossing the creek several more times.

7. At 1.25 miles, cross an old roadbed.

8. At 1.6 miles, enter what feels like an enchanted bamboo forest. This is a great photo opportunity with the family.

9. Exit the bamboo forest and ascend a small hill. The trail can be muddy here at times.

10. Turn left and walk on an old roadbed for 0.15 mile.

11. Turn right to exit the trail and head back to your car, ending the hike.

Did You Know?

Cowpens was a well-known grazing area for cattle before it became the site of a 1780 skirmish where Patriots, including militiamen, defeated pursuing British troops in the space of a single hour. The Battle of Cowpens was a turning point in the American Revolutionary War.

You'll have several creek crossings on Cowpens Nature Trail.

Appendix

Hike Difficulty Index

This quick-reference index categorizes the hikes in this guide by degree of difficulty. The difficulty rating takes into account the effort the hike requires for children, and makes a good starting point for deciding on a family outdoor adventure.

EASY

MODERATE

STRENUOUS

* rated easy to moderate
** rated moderate to strenuous

More Trail Information

Number of Trails per County

Oconee 5
Pickens 4
Greenville 6
Spartanburg 4
Cherokee 1

Distance (round trip)	Hikes
1 mile or less	Oconee Bells Nature Trail
	.... Twin Falls
	.... Glassy Mountain Heritage Preserve
	.... Hagood Mill Nature Trail
	.... Eva Russell Chandler Trail
	.... Blue Trail
	.... Pleasant Ridge Nature Trail
1 to 2 miles...........................	Buzzard Roost Nature Preserve
	.... Natural Bridge Trail
	.... Lake Placid
	.... Bunched Arrowhead
	.... Pacolet River Heritage Preserve
	.... Croft Nature Trail
2 to 3 miles...........................	Station Cove Falls
	.... Pigpen Falls
	.... Bear Cove Trail
	.... Mountain Creek Trail
	.... Cowpens Nature Trail
3 miles or more	Peters Creek Nature Preserve
	.... Edwin M. Griffin Nature Preserve

Index

W

Notes

Notes

Notes

Milestone Press

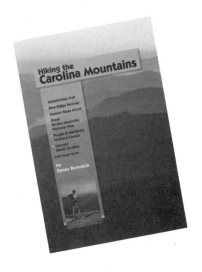

Hiking

- Hiking the
  Carolina Mountains
  by Danny Bernstein

- Hiking North Carolina's
  Blue Ridge Mountains
  by Danny Bernstein

- Day Hiking the
  North Georgia Mountains
  by Jim Parham

- Waterfall Hikes of
  Upstate South Carolina
  by Thomas E. King

- Waterfall Hikes of
  North Georgia
  by Jim Parham

- Family Hikes in
  Upstate South Carolina
  by Scott Lynch

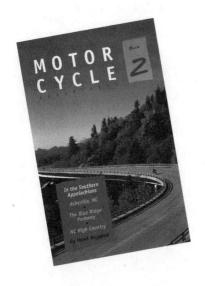

Motorcycle Adventure Series

by Hawk Hagebak

1–*Southern Appalachians: North GA, East TN, Western NC*

2–*Southern Appalachians: Asheville, NC, Blue Ridge Parkway, NC Highcountry*

3–*Central Appalachians: Virginia's Blue Ridge, Shenandoah Valley, West Virginia Highlands*

Off the Beaten Track Mountain Bike Series

by Jim Parham

- Vol. 1: WNC–*Smokies*
- Vol. 2: WNC–*Pisgah*
- Vol. 3: N. *Georgia*
- Vol. 4: E. *Tennessee*
- Vol. 5: N. *Virginia*

Milestone Press

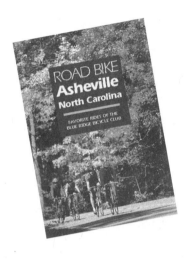 

Road Bike Series

- Road Bike Asheville, NC:
  Favorite Rides of the
  Blue Ridge Bicycle Club
  by The Blue Ridge Bicycle Club

- Road Bike North Georgia:
  25 Great Rides in the Mountains
  and Valleys of North Georgia
  by Jim Parham

- Road Bike the Smokies
  by Jim Parham

Family Adventure

- Natural Adventures
  in the Mountains
  of North Georgia
  by Mary Ellen Hammond
  & Jim Parham